1 MONTH OF
FREE
READING

at

www.ForgottenBooks.com

By purchasing this book you are eligible for one month membership to ForgottenBooks.com, giving you unlimited access to our entire collection of over 1,000,000 titles via our web site and mobile apps.

To claim your free month visit:

www.forgottenbooks.com/free955047

ISBN 978-0-260-54154-3
PIBN 10955047

Forgotten Books is a registered trademark of FB &c Ltd.
Copyright © 2018 FB &c Ltd.
FB &c Ltd, Dalton House, 60 Windsor Avenue, London, SW19 2RR.
Company number 08720141. Registered in England and Wales.

For support please visit www.forgottenbooks.com

S'ECOND BIENNIAL EXHIBITION

PART TWO — WATERCOLORS

★ ★ ★ AND PASTELS ★ ★ ★

FEBRUARY 18 TO MARCH 18, 1936

WHITNEY MUSEUM ★ ★ ★

★ ★ ★ OF AMERICAN ART

TEN WEST EIGHTH STREET · NEW YORK

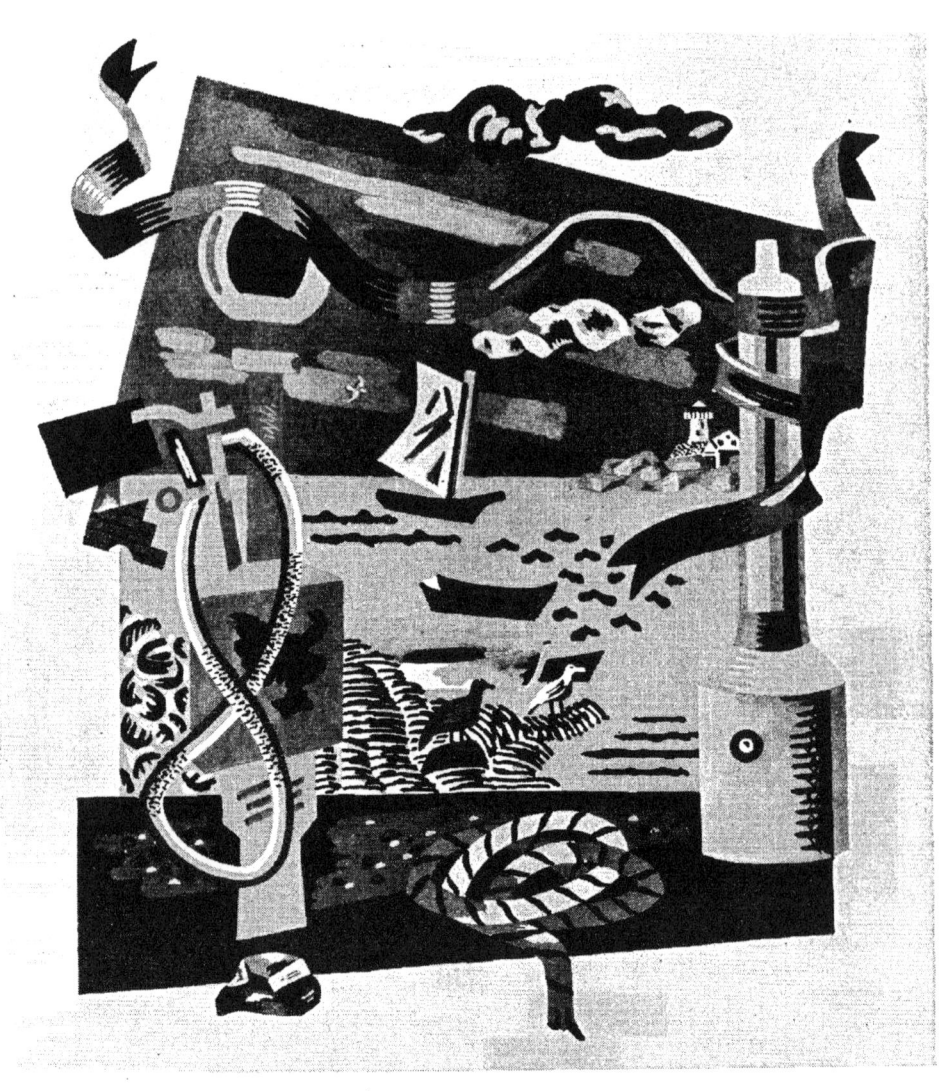

STUART DAVIS
GASOLINE PUMPS

SECOND BIENNIAL EXHIBITION

PART TWO WATERCOLORS AND PASTELS

FEBRUARY 18 TO MARCH 18 · 1936

WHITNEY MUSEUM
OF AMERICAN ART

10 WEST EIGHTH STREET · NEW YORK

F O R E W O R D

THE WHITNEY MUSEUM OF AMERICAN ART
in holding its Second Biennial Exhibition of Contemporary American Sculpture, Watercolors and Prints, has departed from its
original plan inaugurated in 1932 by dividing the exhibition into
two consecutive parts. The first of these, held from January
14th to February 13th, was devoted to sculpture, drawings and
prints; the second and present exhibition is comprised of works
in watercolor, gouache and pastel. This division of the exhibition has made it possible to include two hundred and eight
works in the present showing, which is an increase of eighty-
four over the first watercolor exhibition.

The Museum has at its disposal the sum of twenty thousand
dollars which may be expended for the acquisition of works of
outstanding excellence from the exhibition, including Parts I
and II.

We believe that the exhibition represents in a broad way the
most notable characteristics of American painting in watercolor
and pastel media of today. Our thanks are extended to the
exhibiting artists for their generous co-operation.

NOTE:

MOST OF THE WORKS IN THIS
EXHIBITION ARE FOR SALE. FOR PRICES
AND INFORMATION, VISITORS ARE
REQUESTED TO INQUIRE AT THE
INFORMATION DESK. NO COMMISSION
IS CHARGED BY THE MUSEUM ON
SALES MADE.

CATALOGUE
WATER COLORS
AND PASTELS

GALLERIES I TO VI · FIRST & SECOND FLOORS

E D W A R D   H O P P E R
HOUSE ON PAMET RIVER

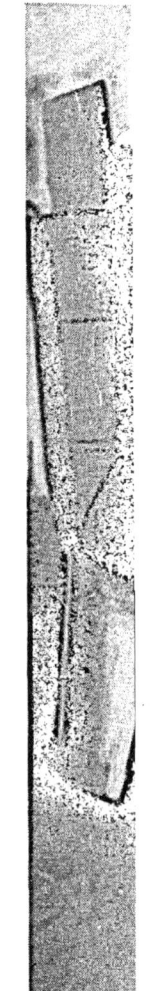

ABRAHAM HARRITON · NEW YORK WATER FRONT

SECOND BALCONY
GEORGES SCHREIBER

NAMES AND ADDRESSES OF ARTISTS REPRESENTED IN THE EXHIBITION AND CATALOGUE NUMBERS OF PICTURES

ARTIST	ADDRESS	Catalogue Numbers
ARONSON, BORIS	433 Central Park, W., N. Y. C.	1, 2
AVERY, MILTON	212 E. 65th St., N. Y. C.	3, 4
BAKOS, JOZEF G.	Santa Fe, N. M.	5, 6
BASKERVILLE, CHARLES.	36 E. 57th St., N. Y. C..	7, 8
BEAL, REYNOLDS	Rockport, Mass.	9, 10
BELL, CECIL C.	19 E. 9th St., N. Y. C.	11, 12
BIDDLE, GEORGE	1712 N St., N. W., Wash., D. C.	13, 14
BLANCH, LUCILE	Woodstock, Ulster Co., N. Y.	15, 16
BLOCH, JULIUS	10 So. 18th St., Phila, Pa.	17, 18
BOHLMAN, EDGAR	31 E. 30th St., N. Y. C.	19, 20
BOHROD, AARON	2406 N. Clark St., Chicago, Ill.	21, 22
BOWES, ARTHUR	2321 Prospect Ave., Bronx, N. Y. C.	23, 24
BOYD, FISKE	55 Hobart Ave., Summit, N. J.	25, 26
BRITTON, EDGAR	511 Grant Pl., Chicago, Ill.	27, 28
BURCHFIELD, CHARLES E.	Box 78, Gardenville, N. Y.	29, 30
BURKHARD, HENRI	Box 196, Fort Lee, N. J.	31, 32
BURWASH, NATHANIEL C.	313 E. 13th St., N. Y. C.	33, 34
CARTER, CLARENCE H.	2074 E. 107th St., Cleveland, O.	35, 36
CHAPIN, FRANCIS	237 Menomonee St., Chicago, Ill.	37, 38
COOLEY, LYDIA	219 W. 14th St., N. Y. C.	39, 40
CORCOS, LUCILLE	121 Joralemon St., Brooklyn, N. Y.	41, 42
DALSTROM, GUSTAF	649 Kemper Pl., Chicago, Ill.	43, 44
DASBURG, ANDREW	Taos, N. M.	45, 46
DAVEY, RANDALL	Canyon Road, Santa Fe, N. M.	47, 48
DAVIS, STUART	43—7th Ave., N. Y. C.	49, 50
DAY, HORACE	301 Henry St., N. Y. C.	51, 52
DEHNER, WALT	Whitehouse, Ohio	53, 54
DIRK, NATHANIEL	9 W. 14th St., N. Y. C.	55, 56
DODDS, PEGGY	641—14th Ave., Paterson, N. J.	57, 58
DOHANOS, STEVAN	19 Huron Rd., Tuckahoe, N. Y.	59, 60
DONNELLY, THOMAS	Box 99, Valhalla, N. Y.	61, 62
DOWDEN, RAYMOND BAXTER	345 W. 4th St., N. Y. C.	63, 64
DRIGGS, ELSIE	13 W. 9th St., N. Y. C.	65, 66
EDIE, STUART	98 Charlton St., N. Y. C.	67, 68
EILSHEMIUS, LOUIS M.	118 E. 57th St, N. Y. C.	69, 70
FERSTADT, LOUIS G.	242 E. 19th St., N. Y. C.	71, 72
FIENE, ERNEST	c/o Downtown Gallery, 113 W. 13th St., N. Y. C.	73, 74
FRANKLIN, GEORGE	Bearsville, Ulster Co., N. Y.	75, 76
FRAZIER, SUSAN	165 E. 83rd St., N. Y. C.	77, 78
FREE, KARL	14 W. 8th St., N. Y. C.	79
GANSO, EMIL	Woodstock, Ulster Co., N. Y.	80, 81

GOTTLIEB, HARRY	6 E. 14th St., N. Y. C.	82, 83
GREITZER, JACK J.	1763 Page Ave., Cleveland, Ohio	84, 85
GROSZ, GEORGE	40-41—221st St., Bayside, L. I., N. Y.	86, 87
HARNLY, PERKINS	353 W. 27th St., N. Y.	88, 89
HARRITON, ABRAHAM	3908—48th ST., Sunnyside, L. I., N.	90, 91
HARTLEY, MARSDEN	227 E. 60th ST., N. Y.	92, 93
HARTMAN, BERTRAM	240 E. 20th St., N. Y.	94, 95
HERING, HARRY	8507 Norwich Ave., Jamaica, L. I., N.	96, 97
HIGGINS, EUGENE	360 W. 22nd St., N. Y.	98, 99
HOLZHAUER, EMIL	51 W. 10th St., N. Y. C.	100, 101
HOPPER, EDWARD	3 Washington Sq., No. N. Y.	102
HORTER, EARL	2219 DeLancey St., Phila, Pa.	103, 104
HOWARD, LORETTA	Maxwelton, Dayton, Ohio	105, 106
IVES, NEIL McDOWELL	Woodstock, Ulster Co., N. Y.	107, 108
KAESELAU, CHARLES	Provincetown, Mass.	109, 110
KELLER, HENRY G.	1381 Addison Rd., Cleveland, Ohio	111, 112
KELPE, PAUL	229 W. 20th ST., N. Y. C.	113, 114
KLITGAARD, GEORGINA	Bearsville, Ulster Co., N. Y.	115, 116
KLONIS, STEWART	26-35 Fourth St., Astoria, L. I., N. Y.	117, 118
KNATHS, KARL	8 Commercial ST., Provincetown, Mass.	119, 120
LEVER, HAYLEY	66 Ravine Ave., Caldwell, N. J.	121, 122
LIBERTE, L. JEAN	10 E. 15th St., N. Y. C.	123, 124
LOCKWOOD, WARD	Taos, N. M.	125, 126
LONERGAN, JOHN	140 W. 71st St., N. Y. C.	127, 128
MARGOLIES, S. L.	104-27—197th St., Hollis, L. I., N. Y.	129, 130
MARIN, JOHN	243 Clark Terrace, Cliffside, N. J.	131, 132
MARSH, REGINALD	4 E. 12th St., N. Y. C.	133, 134
MATULKA, JAN	439 E. 89th St., N. Y. C.	135, 136
McAUSLAN, HELEN	12 E. 15th St., N. Y. C.	137, 138
McCOSH, DAVID	967 Patterson St., Eugene, Oregon	139, 140
MECKLEM, AUSTIN	Woodstock, Ulster Co., N. Y.	141, 142
MEYEROWITZ, WILLIAM	54 W. 74th St., N. Y. C.	143, 144
MITCHELL, BRUCE	126 E. 28th St., N. Y. C.	145, 146
ORR, ELLIOT	Box 404, Chappaqua, N. Y.	147, 148
PERKINS, HARLEY	104 Revere St., Boston, Mass.	149, 150
PICKEN, GEORGE	518 E. 85th St., N. Y. C.	151, 152
PITTMAN, HOBSON	57 S. Eagle Rd., Manoa, Upper Darby, Pa.	153, 154
REISMAN, PHILIP	62 W. 37th St., N. Y. C.	155, 156
RIBAK, LOUIS	227 Lewis St., N. Y. C.	157, 158
ROHLAND, CAROLINE SPEARE	Woodstock, Ulster Co., N. Y.	159, 160
ROHLAND, PAUL	Woodstock, Ulster Co., N. Y.	161, 162
ROSS, SANFORD	140 E. 72nd St., N. Y. C.	163, 164
SAMPLE, PAUL S.	676 La Loma Rd., Pasadena, Calif.	165, 166
SCHARY, SAUL	47 E. 9th St., N. Y. C.	167, 168

ARTIST	ADDRESS	Catalogue Numbers
SCHNAKENBERG, H. E.	601 West End Ave., N. Y. C.	169, 170
SCHREIBER, GEORGES	145 W. 14th St., N. Y. C.	171, 172
SHEETS, MILLARD	532 W. 10th St., Claremont, Calif.	173, 174
SIMPSON, MARTHA	430 W. 57th St., N. Y. C.	175, 176
SMITH, ALICE R. HUGER	69 Church St., Charleston, S. C.	177, 178
SMITH, JACOB GETLAR	63 E. 57th St., N. Y. C.	179, 180
SOKOLE, MIRON	57 W. 8th St., N. Y. C.	181, 182
SOYER, MOSES	240 W. 4th St., N. Y. C.	183, 184
SPRINCHORN, CARL	12 Sutton Pl., No., N. Y. C.	185, 186
STEIGER, HARWOOD	150 W. 4th St., N. Y. C.	187, 188
STELLA, JOSEPH	2431 Southern Blvd., Bronx, N. Y. C.	189, 190
TODD, ANNE OPHELIA	345 W. 4th St., N. Y. C.	191, 192
TRUNK, JR., HERMAN	135 Essex St., Brooklyn, N. Y.	193, 194
TUCKER, ALLEN	106 E. 85th St., N. Y. C.	195, 196
VAN VEEN, STUYVESANT	24 W. 96th St., N. Y. C.	197, 198
WALKOWITZ, ABRAHAM	1469—53rd St., Brooklyn, N. Y.	199, 200
WEBER, MAX	10 Hartley Rd., Great Neck, L. I., N. Y.	201, 202
WHITNEY, ISABEL L.	Hotel Berkeley, 20 Fifth Ave., N. Y. C.	203, 204
WHORF, JOHN	c/o Milch Galleries, 108 W. 57th St., N. Y. C.	205, 206
ZORACH, WILLIAM	17 W. 9th St., N. Y. C.	207, 208

WHITNEY MUSEUM PUBLICATIONS
AMERICAN ARTISTS SERIES

GEORGE BELLOWS.....................*George W. Eggers*
ALEXANDER BROOK...........*Edward Alden Jewell*
MARY CASSATT.....................*Forbes Watson*
GLENN O. COLEMAN...........*C. Adolph Glassgold*
ARTHUR B. DAVIES.....................*Royal Cortissoz*
CHARLES DEMUTH.....................*William Murrell*
GUY PÈNE DU BOIS.....................*Royal Cortissoz*
WILLIAM GLACKENS.................*Guy Pène du Bois*
ROBERT HENRI.....................*Helen Appleton Read*
EDWARD HOPPER.....................*Guy Pène du Bois*
BERNARD KARFIOL.....................*Jean Paul Slusser*
ERNEST LAWSON.....................*Guy Pène du Bois*
GEORGE LUKS.................*Elisabeth Luther Cary*
HENRY LEE MCFEE.....................*Virgil Barker*
KENNETH HAYES MILLER...........*Alan Burroughs*
MAURICE PRENDERGAST...........*Margaret Breuning*
H. E. SCHNAKENBERG.....................*Lloyd Goodrich*
JOHN SLOAN.....................*Guy Pène du Bois*
EUGENE SPEICHER.....*Frank Jewett Mather, Jr.*
ALLEN TUCKER.....................*Forbes Watson*
JOHN TWACHTMAN.....................*Allen Tucker*

Each volume contains a critical essay by an authoritative writer on art, a short biography, a bibliography and twenty full-page reproductions. Each volume $2.00

CATALOGUE OF THE COLLECTION . . . $5.00 a copy

A brochure entitled A CRITICAL INTRODUCTION TO AMERICAN PAINTING by Virgil Barker . . 60c a copy

THOMAS EAKINS by Lloyd Goodrich . . . $10.00 a copy

A HISTORY OF AMERICAN GRAPHIC HUMOR
by William Murrell
Volume I . . . . $5.00 a copy
Volume II in preparation

ON SALE AT THE BOOK STALL

THE WHITNEY MUSEUM OF AME

IS OPEN
FREE TO T
DAILY EXC
FROM 1 P. M

★ ★ ★ ★ ★ ★ ★ ★ ★ ★ ★ ★ ★ ★ ★

PRINTED BY L. F.

CPSIA information can be obtained
at www.ICGtesting.com
Printed in the USA
BVHW041120211218
536175BV00005B/18/P